ALEX KAI

BOOK

How a curious kid Used Smart Ideas to Help the World

Owens JK. Publications

THIS BOOK BELONGS TO

NAME :

ONCE UPON A TIME, IN A BUSTLING CITY CALLED NEW YORK, THERE LIVED A CURIOUS YOUNG BOY NAMED ALEX KARP

FROM A VERY YOUNG AGE, ALEX LOVED ASKING QUESTIONS. "WHY IS THE SKY BLUE? HOW DO AIRPLANES FLY? WHAT MAKES ICE CREAM SO DELICIOUS?" HIS CURIOUS MIND WAS ALWAYS AT WORK, EXPLORING THE WORLD AROUND HIM.

After school, Alex had a great idea! He wanted to help organizations make better decisions using technology

As he grew older, Alex found himself fascinated by computers. He was amazed at how people could use these magical machines to create videos, write stories

Copyright©Owens JK. Publications
2024

All Rights reserved .No part of this publication may be reproduced,redistributed or transmitted in any form or by any means including photocopying ,recording ,or other electronic or mechanical methods without the prior permission of the publisher ,expect in the case of brief quotations embodied in critical reviews and certain other non commercial uses permitted by copyright law.

Who Should Read This Book

Young Readers (Ages 7-13):

The book is designed for children and pre-teens who are curious about technology, business, and how these two areas interact in the modern world. It provides fun and engaging insights suitable for this age group.

Parents and Educators:

Parents looking for educational materials to inspire their children can benefit from this book. Educators can use it as a resource to teach students about technology and its impact on society and business.

Aspiring Young Entrepreneurs:

Kids who dream of starting their own businesses or who are interested in becoming inventors will find valuable information and inspiration to pursue their goals.

Students in STEM Programs:

Students interested in science, technology, engineering, and mathematics (STEM) will gain a broader understanding of how technology influences different industries.

Curious Minds:

Anyone with a general interest in learning about technology, business, and innovation will enjoy the engaging stories and fun facts presented in the book.

Caution

Complexity of Topics:

While the book simplifies many concepts, some ideas may still be challenging for younger readers to fully grasp. Parents or educators may need to provide additional explanations or context.

Rapidly Changing Technology:

The technology landscape evolves quickly, and some information may become outdated. Readers should stay curious and seek out new information to keep up with technological advancements.

Screen Time Awareness:

The book discusses various technologies that can involve screen time. Parents should encourage a balanced approach to technology use and monitor the amount of time their children spend on devices.

Real-World Application:

While the book presents exciting ideas about technology and business, it's essential for readers to understand that real-world applications require hard work, dedication, and sometimes facing failures.

Encouragement to Explore:

While the book encourages exploration and innovation, young readers should also be reminded that not every idea will succeed and that perseverance is key to overcoming obstacles.

This book is a wonderful resource for young readers interested in the world of technology and business. With guidance from parents and educators, it can spark curiosity and inspire the next generation of innovators and entrepreneurs. By being aware of the cautions outlined, readers can make the most of their learning experience and explore the exciting possibilities that lie ahead

TABLE CONTENT

How Technology Started

Once upon a time, in a world not so different from ours, there was a very curious little caveman named Grog. Grog lived in a cave with his family and had one big dream: to make life easier and more fun! You see, Grog had a lot of problems. His club was too heavy, his cave was too dark, and he always lost his pet saber-toothed kitten, Fluffy!

The First Invention

One day, while sitting on a rock, Grog had an idea! "What if I make my club lighter?" he thought. So, he took a long stick and tied a sharp rock to it. Ta-da! The first spear was born! Grog was so excited that he jumped up and accidentally hit himself on the head. "Ouch!" he yelled, but then he realized he could use the spear to catch fish for dinner instead of chasing them with his heavy club. Grog shouted, "Hooray for inventions!"

Light Up My Life

But Grog had another problem—his cave was as dark as a bottomless pit! He needed a light. So, he and Fluffy decided to collect sticks and stones. After some poking and prodding, they discovered that rubbing two sticks together created fire! "Wow, look at that!" Grog said, jumping back. "Fire! Now I can see my dinner and cook it too!" Fluffy, however, was less impressed and just wanted to chase the flickering flames.

The Wheel-y Great Idea

As time passed, Grog realized that dragging heavy things through the dirt was hard work. One day, while rolling a round stone, he thought, "What if I make something that rolls?" So, he gathered some wood, cut it into circles, and made the first wheel! When he tried it out, he rolled right into a bush! "Whee!" he laughed, poking his head out. The wheel made carrying heavy things so much easier! Suddenly, Grog was the fastest caveman around.

A New Way to Talk

Grog was happy, but he wanted to share his amazing inventions with his friends who lived far away. So, he decided to create drawings on the walls of his cave. He drew pictures of his spear, fire, and wheel. His friend, Wog, saw the drawings and shouted, "What are these funny squiggles?" Grog replied, "They're pictures of my cool inventions!" Soon, everyone started drawing and sharing stories through pictures. It was the beginning of writing!

The Age of Ideas

As years went by, Grog's inventions inspired many other cavemen and cavewomen. They created all sorts of things: clothing made from animal skins, baskets for gathering food, and even a rudimentary version of a telephone made from two cans and a really long string! Grog was amazed by all the creativity. "If we can invent so many things, just think about what the future holds!" he exclaimed.

The Super-Duper Future

Fast forward many, many years, and the world has changed! People invented computers, smartphones, and robots that could even dance! Grog would be so proud of his little cave idea that sparked a million inventions. Fluffy, now a fluffy old cat, still couldn't understand why humans liked those silly computers. "Just give me a sunny spot and a nap!" she would say.

The Lesson of Grog

And so, the story of Grog teaches us that technology started with a curious mind and a desire to solve problems. Every great invention begins with an idea, and who knows? Maybe one day, you'll create something that will change the world too! Just remember to keep asking questions, experimenting, and, of course, having fun along the way!

And that, dear reader, is how technology started—with a curious caveman, a lot of laughs, and a sprinkle of creativity!

CHAPTER 1: The Tech Wizard

Once upon a time, in a bustling city called New York, there lived a curious young boy named Alex Karp. Little did he know that one day, he would become a famous tech wizard, making the world a better place with his brilliant ideas!

A Curious Kid

From a very young age, Alex loved asking questions. "Why is the sky blue? How do airplanes fly? What makes ice cream so delicious?" His curious mind was always at work, exploring the world around him. While other kids played with toys, Alex took apart his toys to see how they worked. Sometimes, he even put them back together— though sometimes they were a little worse for wear!

Learning and Growing

As he grew older, Alex found himself fascinated by computers. He was amazed at how people could use these magical machines to create videos, write stories, and even connect with friends from all around the world! "If only I could use a computer to solve big problems!" he thought.

So, he decided to learn everything he could about technology. He studied hard in school and even went to university, where he learned about computer science and engineering.

The Birth of an Idea

After school, Alex had a great idea! He wanted to help organizations make better decisions using technology.

"What if I create something that could help them understand their data?" he wondered. With that thought, he co-founded a company called Palantir.

Now, what is Palantir, you ask? Think of it like a super-duper magnifying glass for data! It helps people see patterns and understand information that's hidden away, just like a detective solving a mystery. Whether it's helping governments keep people safe or assisting businesses in making smarter choices, Palantir became a powerful tool for good.

Adventures in Technology

As the years went by, Alex Karp, the tech wizard, went on many adventures. He traveled around the world, meeting incredible people who used his technology to tackle huge challenges. One day, he helped a team of scientists track endangered animals to keep them safe from poachers. On another occasion, he helped firefighters use data to respond quickly to wildfires.

Alex always believed that technology should help make the world a better place. "We can use our skills to solve problems that really matter!" he would say with a big smile.

The Fun Side of Alex

But Alex wasn't all about serious work! He loved to have fun too. He often told silly jokes to his team at Palantir to keep everyone laughing. "Why did the computer go to the doctor?" he would ask. "Because it had a virus!" Everyone would burst into laughter, and suddenly, the office was filled with joy.

He also enjoyed playing games and encouraging kids to be curious. "If you have an idea, don't be afraid to share it!" he would tell young innovators. "Every great invention starts with a simple thought!"

Inspiring Future Innovators

Today, Alex Karp is not just known as a tech wizard but also as a role model for young minds everywhere. He teaches kids that being curious, asking questions, and believing in themselves can lead to amazing discoveries.

"Remember," he says, "you can change the world, one idea at a time!"

And so, the story of Alex Karp reminds us that with curiosity, hard work, and a sprinkle of fun, we can all be a little like him—tech wizards ready to take on the world!

So, what are you waiting for? Start exploring, ask questions, and who knows? You might just create something extraordinary!

Fun Facts About Alex Karp

Born to Explore: Alex was born in 1967 in New York City, but he grew up in a small town in Pennsylvania. Even as a kid, he loved exploring new ideas and learning how things worked!

A Love for Books: Alex is a big fan of reading! He believes that books are a gateway to knowledge and imagination. He often reads about history, technology, and philosophy.

An Adventurous Spirit: While studying at college, Alex traveled all over the world. He loves experiencing different cultures, meeting new people, and learning from their stories.

Tech Wizard: Alex co-founded Palantir Technologies in 2003. Palantir helps companies and governments use data to solve problems and make smart decisions. It's like having a superpower for understanding information!

Silly at Heart: Alex loves to keep things fun at work! He often shares jokes and funny stories with his team to create a happy and creative atmosphere. Laughter is one of his favorite tools!

Champion of Curiosity: Alex believes that curiosity is the key to innovation. He encourages kids to ask questions and explore their interests, no matter how silly they might seem. "If you can dream it, you can do it!" he says.

Outdoor Enthusiast: When he's not working on tech, Alex enjoys spending time outdoors. Whether hiking, biking, or just relaxing in nature, he loves to connect with the world around him.

A Friend to Animals: Alex is passionate about wildlife conservation. He uses Palantir's technology to help protect endangered species and their habitats. Saving animals is one of his superhero missions!

Role Model for Kids: Alex often speaks at schools and events to inspire young people. He shares his journey and encourages them to follow their dreams. "Never stop believing in yourself!" he always reminds them.

Curly Hair, Don't Care: Alex has a unique hairstyle that makes him stand out! His curly hair is often a conversation starter, and he embraces his fun look with pride.

A Global Impact: Palantir is used by organizations worldwide to tackle important challenges, from disaster response to healthcare. Alex's work is making a difference across the globe!

Loves to Learn: Alex is always trying to learn new things, whether it's about technology, art, or science. He believes that learning never stops and encourages everyone to keep growing.

CHAPTER 2: The Journey Begins

Alex Karp's Early Life

Alex Karp was born on October 3, 1967, in New York City. From the very beginning, he was a curious and imaginative child, always asking questions and looking for answers. Let's take a journey through his early life to see how the young Alex became the innovative tech leader he is today!

A Curious Kid

Growing up, Alex was not just an ordinary kid; he was an extraordinary explorer of ideas! His parents encouraged his curiosity, often taking him to museums, art galleries, and science exhibits. Alex loved to learn about everything—from dinosaurs to outer space. He would read books late into the night, dreaming of the amazing things he could discover.

The Move to Pennsylvania

When Alex was still young, his family moved to a small town in Pennsylvania. This change brought a new adventure for him. In the quiet countryside, Alex spent time exploring nature and the great outdoors. He would go on long walks, collect interesting rocks, and study the plants and animals around him. This love for exploration and discovery continued to grow, shaping his future pursuits.

A Passion for Learning

In school, Alex stood out as a bright student. He loved subjects like math and science, where he could solve puzzles and experiment with ideas. However, he was also drawn to the arts and philosophy, exploring how creativity and critical thinking could come together. His teachers often praised him for his inquisitive nature, and he never hesitated to share his thoughts in class.

A Young Innovator

As a teenager, Alex became fascinated with technology. He spent hours tinkering with computers, coding programs, and trying to understand how technology worked. While other kids played video games, he was busy creating his own! His interest in technology ignited a passion for using it to solve real-world problems.

Education and Growth

After high school, Alex attended Haverford College in Pennsylvania, where he studied philosophy and political science. He wanted to understand the world better, exploring the connections between technology, society, and human behavior. He then went on to earn a doctorate in social science from Stanford University. Here, he further developed his ideas about how technology could be used to improve people's lives.

A Vision for the Future

During his studies, Alex began to see the potential for technology to tackle big challenges. He believed that data could unlock solutions to problems that affected people around the world. This vision led him to co-found Palantir Technologies in 2003, a company that focuses on helping organizations make sense of data and use it for good.

Alex Karp's early life was filled with curiosity, creativity, and a passion for learning. From exploring nature in Pennsylvania to studying philosophy and technology, these experiences shaped him into the innovative leader he is today. Alex's journey shows us that with curiosity, hard work, and a little imagination, anyone can achieve their dreams and make a positive impact on the world!

Growing Up in Pennsylvania

After spending his early childhood in New York City, Alex Karp's family moved to a small town in Pennsylvania. This new place would become the perfect playground for his growing mind. Pennsylvania's wide-open spaces, beautiful forests, and friendly small-town atmosphere gave young Alex a chance to explore the world around him in new and exciting ways!

From the Big City to the Countryside

Moving from the busy streets of New York City to the peaceful countryside of Pennsylvania was a big change for Alex. In the city, he had grown used to the constant hustle and bustle, tall buildings, and noisy cars. But now, he found himself surrounded by rolling hills, open fields, and lots of trees. It was quiet, calm, and perfect for an adventurous kid like Alex.

A Nature Lover

Pennsylvania's nature was like a giant outdoor classroom for Alex. He spent hours wandering through the woods, observing the plants and animals, and letting his curiosity lead the way. He would collect rocks, study the insects he found, and wonder about the mysteries of the natural world. This love for nature made Alex appreciate how everything in the world was connected, just like pieces of a big puzzle.

The Young Explorer

Living in Pennsylvania allowed Alex to stretch his imagination. Without the constant distractions of city life, he found time to think deeply about the world around him. He would often go on long walks, letting his mind wander. During these walks, he thought up new ideas, created stories in his head, and dreamed of how he could make the world a better place.

School Days and Big Questions

At school, Alex was a bit different from the other kids. While many of them were interested in sports and games, Alex was fascinated by ideas. He loved to ask big questions, like "Why do things work the way they do?" and "How can we make life better for everyone?" His teachers noticed his passion for learning and encouraged him to keep asking questions.

Alex's school in Pennsylvania was smaller than the schools in New York City, but he enjoyed the close-knit community. He got to know his teachers and classmates well, and everyone appreciated his unique way of looking at the world. Even though he didn't always fit in with everyone else, Alex never stopped being curious and never stopped exploring.

Tinkering with Technology

While nature filled his days, Alex's love for technology was growing too. He would spend his free time taking apart gadgets and learning how they worked. Whether it was an old radio or a broken toy, Alex was determined to understand how every little piece fit together. His parents supported his curiosity, even if it meant their house was sometimes filled with wires, batteries, and tools!

This early tinkering with technology would lay the foundation for his future as a tech innovator. Alex didn't know it yet, but his love for solving problems with technology would one day lead him to co-found a company that would change the way the world worked.

Lessons from Pennsylvania

Growing up in Pennsylvania taught Alex many important lessons. It taught him to appreciate the simple things in life, like a quiet walk in the woods or the beauty of a starry night. It also taught him the value of hard work and persistence. Whether he was building something new or figuring out how to fix something, Alex learned that patience and determination were key to solving problems. Most importantly, living in Pennsylvania gave Alex the time and space to dream big. He didn't let the quiet countryside hold him back. Instead, he used it as a place to grow his ideas and his imagination.

CHAPTER 3: The Big Idea

What is Palantir?

Imagine you have a big box of puzzles. Each piece is different, and they all fit together to create a complete picture. Now, think of a company that helps people put those puzzle pieces together using technology. That company is called Palantir!

A Special Kind of Company

Palantir Technologies was started in 2003 by a group of smart people, including Alex Karp. They wanted to create tools that could help organizations understand and use their data better. But what is data? Well, data is information! It can be numbers, words, pictures, or anything that gives us knowledge about the world. Just like the pieces of a puzzle, when you put data together in the right way, it can help you see the bigger picture!

Helping Different Organizations

Palantir works with many different organizations, from the government to private companies. Here's how it helps them:

Solving Big Problems: Sometimes, organizations face big challenges, like figuring out how to keep people safe or helping people find missing persons. Palantir's tools can analyze lots of data to help them come up with solutions. It's like being a detective and using clues to solve a mystery!

Making Smart Decisions: Companies need to make important decisions every day. Palantir helps them look at their data to see what's working and what's not. This way, they can choose the best paths to take, just like choosing the best route on a treasure map!

Working Together: Palantir's tools allow different people in an organization to work together better. Imagine a big team trying to build a giant Lego castle. If everyone knows what their job is and can see how their pieces fit together, they can build something amazing!

How Palantir Works

Palantir has two main products called Palantir Gotham and Palantir Foundry. Each one is like a superhero in the world of data!

Palantir Gotham: This tool is mainly used by government agencies, like the police or the military. It helps them find patterns in data that can keep people safe. For example, Gotham can help track down bad guys by analyzing information from different sources, like phone calls or social media. It's like having a superpower to see what others can't!

Palantir Foundry: This tool is for companies in various industries, such as healthcare, finance, and manufacturing. Foundry helps these companies understand their data and improve their services. For instance, a hospital might use Foundry to figure out how to provide better care for patients by analyzing health data.

Why Is Palantir Important?

Palantir is important because it helps organizations make better choices and solve problems that affect people's lives. Whether it's saving lives, protecting people, or helping companies grow, Palantir plays a big role in making the world a better place.

A Focus on Privacy

One cool thing about Palantir is that it cares about privacy. It knows that not everyone wants their data shared, and it makes sure to keep information safe and secure. It's like a superhero protecting people's secrets!

Fun Fact!

Did you know that the name "Palantir" comes from a magical stone in The Lord of the Rings? In the story, the palantir allows people to see things far away. Just like in the story, Palantir Technologies helps organizations see and understand important information from far and wide!

How Alex Karp Started His Company

Alex Karp's journey to starting Palantir Technologies is an exciting story of creativity, determination, and a passion for solving big problems! Let's take a look at how he turned his ideas into a successful company that helps organizations understand and use data.

The Idea Spark

It all began when Alex was studying at Stanford University. He was fascinated by how technology could be used to solve real-world problems. He noticed that many organizations had tons of data but didn't know how to use it effectively. It was like having a treasure chest full of gold coins but not knowing how to open it!

Alex wanted to create a way for organizations to unlock their data treasure and use it to make better decisions. This idea sparked his interest in creating a company that could help with that.

Gathering a Team

But Alex knew he couldn't do it alone. To turn his idea into reality, he needed a team of talented and creative people who shared his vision. He began reaching out to friends and other smart individuals who were passionate about technology and problem-solving.

In 2003, Alex, along with his co-founders—Peter Thiel, Joe Lonsdale, and others—came together to form Palantir Technologies.

CHAPTER 4: A Day in the Life

What Does Alex Karp Do?

Alex Karp is a busy and important person, and he wears many hats at Palantir Technologies! Let's explore what his job involves and how he makes a difference in the world through his work.

1. Chief Executive Officer (CEO)

As the CEO of Palantir, Alex is the leader of the company. This means he is in charge of making big decisions that guide the direction of the business. He works with his team to set goals and create plans to achieve them. Just like a captain leads a ship, Alex leads Palantir toward success!

2. Innovator and Visionary

Alex is not just a leader; he is also an innovator. He loves to think about new ideas and how technology can be used to solve complex problems. His creative mind helps shape the products and services that Palantir offers. He encourages his team to think outside the box and come up with fresh solutions that can help organizations make sense of their data.

3. Problem Solver

One of Alex's main goals is to help organizations tackle their biggest challenges. He believes that data can unlock answers to tough questions. In his role, he works closely with customers to understand their needs and figure out how Palantir's tools can help them. It's like being a detective who helps others find the clues they need to solve their mysteries!

4. Advocate for Data Privacy

Alex cares deeply about the importance of data privacy and security. He wants to make sure that the information organizations use is kept safe and that people's privacy is respected. As a leader, he speaks out about the need for responsible data usage and ensures that Palantir's tools protect users' information. Think of him as a superhero who guards people's secrets!

5. Public Speaker and Educator

Alex often shares his ideas and thoughts about technology and data through public speaking. He attends conferences and events where he talks about the future of technology, how it can be used for good, and the challenges that come with it. By educating others about these important topics, he inspires the next generation of thinkers and innovators.

6. Collaborator

Working with other talented people is important to Alex. He collaborates with a wide range of individuals, from engineers and designers at Palantir to leaders in various industries. This teamwork helps create better products and solutions that can meet the needs of their customers.

7. Futurist

Alex often thinks about the future and how technology will continue to evolve. He imagines a world where data can help solve big problems like healthcare, safety, and environmental challenges. By envisioning this future, he helps guide Palantir to stay at the forefront of technology and innovation.

Meetings, Ideas, and Teamwork at Palantir

At Palantir Technologies, meetings, ideas, and teamwork are at the heart of everything they do! These elements help create a dynamic environment where creativity thrives and solutions to big problems are born. Let's dive into how Alex Karp and his team make magic happen through collaboration!

1. The Power of Meetings

Meetings are an essential part of how Palantir operates. They are not just boring sessions where people sit and talk; they are exciting opportunities for sharing ideas and brainstorming solutions. During these meetings, team members gather to discuss projects, share updates, and brainstorm new concepts. Here's how they make the most out of meetings:

Sharing Ideas: Team members are encouraged to bring their ideas to the table. Whether it's a small suggestion or a big concept, every idea is welcomed. This creates an environment where everyone feels valued and empowered to contribute.

Problem-Solving Together: When challenges arise, meetings provide a space for the team to come together and tackle them. They brainstorm solutions, analyze data, and work collaboratively to find the best paths forward.

Setting Goals: Meetings help the team align on goals and priorities. By discussing what needs to be done, everyone knows their role and what they should focus on. This teamwork helps Palantir stay organized and effective!

2. A Hub for Ideas

At Palantir, ideas flow like a river! The company fosters a culture of creativity and innovation, where thinking outside the box is encouraged. Here's how they cultivate a hub for ideas:

Open Communication: Team members communicate openly and honestly with each other. This creates a supportive atmosphere where individuals feel comfortable sharing their thoughts without fear of criticism.

Diverse Perspectives: Palantir values diversity in its team. When people from different backgrounds and experiences come together, they bring unique viewpoints that spark new ideas. This mix of perspectives leads to more innovative solutions.

Encouraging Curiosity: Alex and his team promote a curious mindset. They believe that asking questions and exploring new concepts can lead to groundbreaking discoveries. This approach encourages everyone to dig deeper and think critically.

3. Teamwork Makes the Dream Work

Teamwork is the secret ingredient to Palantir's success! Working together allows the team to combine their strengths and talents to create amazing solutions. Here's how teamwork shines at Palantir:

Collaboration: Team members collaborate on projects, combining their skills and knowledge. By working together, they can tackle complex problems and come up with comprehensive solutions. It's like a sports team, where everyone plays their part to win the game!

Supporting Each Other: The team at Palantir looks out for one another. They celebrate each other's successes and support each other during challenges. This sense of camaraderie builds strong relationships and a positive work environment.

Learning and Growing Together: Teamwork also means learning from each other. Team members share their expertise and experiences, helping one another grow and improve. This continuous learning helps everyone become better at what they do.

CHAPTER 5: Making a Difference

How Palantir Helps People

Palantir Technologies is a company that uses cutting-edge technology to help organizations make sense of their data. But how does this help people in their everyday lives? Let's explore the various ways Palantir makes a positive impact on individuals and communities!

1. Keeping Communities Safe

One of Palantir's most important roles is helping government agencies, like police departments and emergency services, keep people safe. Here's how they do it:

Crime Prevention: Palantir's tools allow law enforcement to analyze data related to crime trends and patterns. By understanding where and when crimes are likely to happen, police can take proactive measures to prevent them. It's like having a crystal ball that helps keep neighborhoods secure!

Emergency Response: In times of crisis, such as natural disasters or public health emergencies, Palantir helps agencies coordinate their response efforts. By analyzing data in real-time, they can ensure that resources are deployed quickly and efficiently, saving lives and helping communities recover faster.

2. Improving Healthcare

Palantir also plays a crucial role in the healthcare sector, helping hospitals and healthcare providers deliver better services to patients:

Data Analysis for Better Care: Healthcare providers can use Palantir's tools to analyze patient data and identify trends. This helps doctors understand which treatments are most effective and improve patient care. Imagine a doctor having a super-smart assistant that helps them make the best decisions for their patients!

Public Health Initiatives: Palantir supports public health agencies in tracking diseases and outbreaks. By analyzing data from various sources, they can monitor the spread of illnesses and implement strategies to protect communities. This helps ensure that everyone stays healthy and safe.

3. Supporting Businesses

Palantir's technology is not just for government agencies; it also helps businesses make smart decisions that benefit their customers:

Improving Services: Companies can analyze customer data to understand their needs and preferences better. This allows them to create products and services that truly meet the demands of their customers, making shopping experiences more enjoyable.

Boosting Efficiency: Palantir helps businesses streamline their operations by identifying inefficiencies. When companies run more smoothly, they can save time and resources, which can lead to lower prices for consumers. Everyone benefits when businesses operate efficiently!

4. Empowering Decision-Makers

Leaders and decision-makers in various fields rely on Palantir's tools to make informed choices:

Data-Driven Insights: Palantir provides decision-makers with clear insights from their data. This means they can make choices based on facts rather than guesswork. It's like having a trusty guide who points out the best path to take!

Long-Term Planning: Organizations can use Palantir to plan for the future by analyzing trends and forecasting outcomes. This helps them prepare for challenges ahead and make strategic decisions that benefit everyone.

5. Creating Opportunities for Innovation

Palantir encourages creativity and innovation, which can lead to exciting new solutions that benefit society:

Collaboration with Startups: Palantir partners with startups and innovators to help them develop new technologies. By sharing its expertise, Palantir helps these emerging companies grow and succeed, which can lead to groundbreaking products and services that improve lives.

Educational Initiatives: Palantir is also involved in educational initiatives that help people learn about data and technology. By empowering the next generation of thinkers and innovators, they help create a future filled with possibilities!

Alex Karp's Vision for the Future

Alex Karp, the co-founder and CEO of Palantir Technologies, is a visionary leader who thinks deeply about the future of technology and its impact on society. His ideas and insights inspire not only his team at Palantir but also the broader world of technology and innovation.

Let's explore Alex's vision for the future!

1. Empowering Individuals with Data

Alex believes that data should be accessible to everyone, not just big companies or governments. He envisions a future where individuals and small organizations can harness the power of data to make informed decisions. Here's how he sees this happening:

User-Friendly Tools: Alex wants to create easy-to-use tools that allow people to analyze their own data. Imagine being able to understand your own health, finances, or even your daily habits with just a few clicks! This empowerment can lead to better choices and improved lives.

Transparency and Trust: In Alex's future, organizations will prioritize transparency in how they use data. He believes that people should know how their information is being used and feel confident that their privacy is protected. This trust is essential for building a positive relationship between individuals and organizations.

2. Solving Global Challenges

Alex is passionate about using technology to tackle some of the world's biggest challenges. He believes that by leveraging data, we can find innovative solutions to pressing problems:

Healthcare Innovations: Alex envisions a future where data-driven insights lead to breakthroughs in healthcare. By analyzing vast amounts of health data, researchers can discover new treatments and improve patient outcomes. This could mean longer, healthier lives for people around the world!

Environmental Sustainability: Addressing climate change is a significant part of Alex's vision. He believes that technology can help us understand environmental issues better and develop sustainable practices. By using data to track resource consumption and environmental impact, we can create a healthier planet for future generations.

3. Promoting Responsible Technology Use

As technology continues to advance, Alex emphasizes the importance of using it responsibly. He is concerned about the potential misuse of data and technology and advocates for ethical practices:

Ethics in AI and Data Usage: Alex believes that as artificial intelligence (AI) becomes more prevalent, organizations must prioritize ethical considerations. This includes ensuring that AI systems are fair, transparent, and do not perpetuate biases. By doing so, we can create a future where technology serves everyone equally.

Collaboration Over Competition: In Alex's vision, organizations will work together rather than compete against each other. By collaborating and sharing knowledge, they can develop better solutions for society as a whole. This cooperative spirit can lead to greater innovation and progress.

4. Fostering Education and Learning

Alex understands that education is key to preparing future generations for a rapidly changing world. He envisions a future where learning is accessible and encourages curiosity and critical thinking:

Promoting Data Literacy: Alex wants to ensure that everyone has the skills to understand and analyze data. By promoting data literacy in schools and communities, individuals can become informed decision-makers who can navigate the complexities of the modern world.

Encouraging Lifelong Learning: In Alex's future, learning doesn't stop at school. He believes in the importance of lifelong education, where individuals continue to develop new skills throughout their lives. This adaptability will be crucial in a world where technology evolves rapidly.

5. Creating a Better Society Through Technology

At the core of Alex's vision is the belief that technology should enhance our lives and contribute to a better society. He imagines a world where technology fosters connections, understanding, and positive change:

Building Strong Communities: Alex envisions technology as a tool for strengthening communities. By using data to understand local needs and challenges, organizations can develop targeted solutions that improve the quality of life for everyone.

Celebrating Diversity: In Alex's future, diverse voices and perspectives will be valued in the tech industry. He believes that inclusivity leads to more innovative solutions and helps create products that serve a wider range of people. A diverse tech landscape can lead to a richer and more vibrant society.

CHAPTER 6: Overcoming Challenges

The Hard Work Behind Success

Success doesn't come easy, and for Alex Karp, the co-founder and CEO of Palantir Technologies, hard work has been a key ingredient in achieving his goals. Let's explore the dedication, perseverance, and effort that Alex put into building Palantir and what we can learn from his journey!

1. Starting from Scratch

Alex Karp didn't start with a huge company or a lot of resources. He began with an idea and a vision for how technology could change the world. Here's how his journey began:

Identifying a Problem: Alex noticed that many organizations struggled to analyze their data effectively. He saw an opportunity to create software that could help these organizations make sense of their information and use it to make better decisions.

Building a Team: Alex knew he couldn't do it alone. He gathered a small group of talented individuals who shared his vision. They worked together, brainstorming ideas and developing the technology that would become Palantir. This collaborative spirit laid the foundation for the company's success.

2. Facing Challenges Head-On

The road to success is often filled with obstacles, and Alex faced many along the way:

Long Hours and Sacrifices: In the early days of Palantir, Alex and his team worked long hours to develop their software. They often sacrificed personal time and comfort to ensure the company would thrive. This dedication helped them overcome initial hurdles and gain traction in the market.

Learning from Failures: Not every idea worked out perfectly. Alex and his team faced setbacks and challenges that could have discouraged them. Instead, they used these experiences as learning opportunities, adjusting their strategies and improving their technology. This resilience helped them grow stronger.

3. Continuous Innovation

For Alex, hard work isn't just about putting in the hours; it's also about staying innovative and adapting to change:
Listening to Feedback: Alex believes that feedback from users is essential for improvement. He encourages his team to listen to customers and learn from their experiences. By continually refining their products based on feedback, Palantir remains at the forefront of technology.
Investing in Research and Development: To stay ahead of the competition, Alex emphasizes the importance of innovation. Palantir invests in research and development, allowing the company to create new features and technologies that meet the evolving needs of its clients. This commitment to innovation requires hard work and dedication from the entire team.

4. Building a Strong Company Culture

Success is not just about the products; it's also about the people behind them. Alex Karp places a strong emphasis on creating a positive company culture:
Fostering Collaboration: Alex encourages teamwork and collaboration among employees. By creating an environment where everyone feels valued and included, he ensures that employees are motivated to work hard and contribute their best ideas.

Encouraging Growth: Alex believes in the potential of his team members. He invests in their development, providing opportunities for learning and advancement. When employees feel supported and encouraged, they are more likely to work hard and contribute to the company's success.

5. Staying True to Values

Throughout his journey, Alex has remained committed to his core values, which guide his decisions and actions:

Ethical Responsibility: Alex believes that success should not come at the expense of ethics. He emphasizes the importance of using technology responsibly and making decisions that benefit society as a whole.

Long-Term Vision: While many companies focus on short-term gains, Alex maintains a long-term vision for Palantir. He understands that hard work today lays the groundwork for success in the future. This commitment to long-term thinking has helped Palantir navigate challenges and seize opportunities.

Learning from Mistakes

Mistakes are a natural part of life, and they can be some of our greatest teachers! For Alex Karp, co-founder and CEO of Palantir Technologies, learning from mistakes has been a crucial part of his journey to success. Let's dive into how

Alex embraced his mistakes and turned them into valuable lessons!

1. Understanding that Mistakes are Normal

Alex believes that everyone makes mistakes, and it's important to accept that they are a normal part of life. Here's how he views mistakes:

Growth Mindset: Alex encourages a growth mindset, which means believing that abilities can improve through effort and learning. Instead of fearing mistakes, he sees them as opportunities to grow and improve. This mindset allows him and his team to take risks and try new things without being afraid of failure.

Encouraging Openness: At Palantir, Alex fosters an environment where employees feel comfortable admitting their mistakes. This openness helps create a culture of learning, where everyone can share their experiences and learn from one another.

2. Reflecting on Mistakes

When mistakes happen, it's essential to take time to reflect on what went wrong. Alex follows these steps:

Analyzing the Situation: After a mistake occurs, Alex encourages his team to analyze what happened. Was it a decision that was rushed? Did they overlook important information? By understanding the root cause of the mistake, they can learn valuable lessons.

Identifying Key Takeaways: Alex emphasizes the importance of identifying key takeaways from each mistake. What can they do differently next time? By discussing these lessons as a team, they can develop strategies to avoid similar mistakes in the future.

3. Adapting and Innovating

One of the most important aspects of learning from mistakes is the ability to adapt and innovate. Here's how Alex incorporates this into his work:

Being Flexible: Alex knows that the tech industry is constantly changing, and being flexible is crucial. If something doesn't work out, he encourages his team to pivot and try new approaches. This adaptability allows them to stay ahead of the competition and continue to innovate.

Embracing Feedback: Alex values feedback from both his team and clients. When they receive criticism or suggestions, he sees it as a chance to improve. By listening and making changes based on feedback, they can turn mistakes into opportunities for growth.

4. Setting a Positive Example

As a leader, Alex understands the importance of setting a positive example for his team:

Sharing His Own Mistakes: Alex is open about his own mistakes and the lessons he has learned from them. By sharing these experiences, he shows that it's okay to make mistakes and that everyone has room to grow.

Celebrating Learning: Instead of punishing mistakes, Alex celebrates the learning that comes from them. He encourages his team to take calculated risks and view failures as stepping stones toward success. This positive approach helps build confidence and fosters a culture of innovation.

5. Turning Mistakes into Success

Ultimately, Alex believes that learning from mistakes can lead to great success. Here's how this process works:

Building Resilience: Each time Alex and his team learn from a mistake, they become more resilient. They develop the ability to bounce back from setbacks and face challenges with confidence. This resilience is essential for long-term success.

Fueling Innovation: The lessons learned from mistakes often spark new ideas and innovations. Alex encourages his team to think creatively and explore new solutions. By embracing mistakes, they can discover new ways to solve problems and improve their products.

CHAPTER 7: Inspiring Others

Alex's Advice for Young Dreamers

Hey there, young dreamers! Do you have big dreams or ideas that you want to chase? Alex Karp, the co-founder and CEO of Palantir Technologies, has some fantastic advice for you! He believes that anyone can achieve their dreams with the right mindset and dedication. Let's explore some of his key pieces of advice to inspire you on your journey!

1. Believe in Yourself

The first step to achieving your dreams is believing in yourself:

Have Confidence: Alex encourages young dreamers to have confidence in their abilities. Everyone has unique talents and ideas, and you should embrace them! Even when things get tough, remember that you have what it takes to succeed.

Don't Doubt Your Ideas: It's easy to doubt yourself when you have a big idea. Alex says that if you believe in your idea, you should pursue it! Your vision could be the next big thing, so don't be afraid to share it with the world.

2. Embrace Failure as a Teacher

Mistakes are part of the journey, and Alex believes you can learn a lot from them:

Learn from Setbacks: Instead of being discouraged by failure, see it as an opportunity to learn and grow. Every setback can teach you something valuable, helping you improve and move closer to your goals.

Keep Trying: When things don't go as planned, don't give up! Alex reminds us that many successful people have faced challenges before finding success. Keep trying, and remember that perseverance is key!

3. Work Hard and Stay Curious

Hard work and curiosity go hand in hand when pursuing your dreams:

Put in the Effort: Achieving your dreams often requires hard work. Alex believes that dedication and effort can make a significant difference in turning your dreams into reality. Put in the time and energy, and you'll see results!

Stay Curious: Alex encourages young dreamers to stay curious and ask questions. Explore new ideas, learn about different fields, and never stop seeking knowledge.

Curiosity fuels creativity and innovation, helping you think outside the box.

4. Surround Yourself with Great People

The people you choose to be around can impact your journey:

Find Supportive Friends: Surround yourself with friends and mentors who support your dreams and encourage you to be your best self. These positive influences can inspire you and provide guidance along the way.

Learn from Others: Alex believes that everyone has something to teach. Take the time to learn from others, whether they are teachers, family members, or friends. Their experiences and advice can help you navigate your path more effectively.

5. Stay True to Your Values

Alex emphasizes the importance of staying true to your beliefs and values:

Be Ethical: As you pursue your dreams, always act with integrity and kindness. Alex believes that making ethical choices is essential for long-term success. Treat others with respect and fairness, and you'll build strong relationships along the way.

Follow Your Passion: Choose a path that aligns with your passions and interests. When you pursue something you love, you're more likely to stay motivated and committed, even when challenges arise.

6. Dream Big, but Start Small

Dreaming big is important, but it's also essential to take small steps toward your goals:

Set Achievable Goals: Break down your big dreams into smaller, manageable goals. This way, you can track your progress and celebrate your accomplishments along the way!

Take Action: Start taking action today, even if it's just a small step. Whether it's researching your dream career, starting a project, or talking to someone about your ideas, every step counts!

Alex Karp's advice for young dreamers is all about believing in yourself, learning from mistakes, working hard, surrounding yourself with great people, staying true to your values, and dreaming big while taking small steps. Remember, you have the power to turn your dreams into reality. So go out there, embrace your journey, and let your dreams shine bright!

The Importance of Education

Education is one of the most powerful tools in the world. It opens doors, builds opportunities, and helps us understand the world around us. For young dreamers like you, education is not just about sitting in a classroom; it's about learning, growing, and preparing for the future. Let's explore why education is so important!

1. Knowledge is Power

Education provides knowledge, which is essential for understanding the world:

Learning New Things: Through education, you learn about subjects like math, science, history, and art. Each subject gives you important knowledge and skills that can help you in everyday life.

Making Informed Decisions: With education, you can make informed choices. For example, understanding health topics helps you make better choices about what to eat and how to stay active.

2. Developing Critical Thinking Skills

Education helps you develop critical thinking skills, which are crucial for problem-solving:

Analyzing Information: In school, you learn how to analyze information and think critically. This means you can evaluate what you read, hear, or see, and decide whether it makes sense or not.

Solving Problems: Education teaches you how to approach challenges. Whether it's a math problem or a project at school, learning different strategies helps you figure out solutions more effectively.

3. Building Confidence and Self-Esteem

Education can boost your confidence and self-esteem:

Achieving Goals: When you learn something new or achieve a goal in school, it gives you a sense of accomplishment. This feeling can boost your confidence and encourage you to take on new challenges.

Expressing Yourself: Education also helps you express your ideas and opinions. Whether through writing essays or participating in discussions, you learn how to share your thoughts confidently.

4. Opening Up Opportunities

Education is key to unlocking a wide range of opportunities:

Better Job Prospects: Many jobs require a certain level of education. By focusing on your studies, you prepare yourself for a future where you can choose from various career paths.

Higher Earnings: Generally, people with higher levels of education tend to earn more money over their lifetime. This financial stability can lead to a better quality of life and more opportunities for yourself and your family.

5. Promoting Personal Growth

Education is not just about academics; it also promotes personal growth:

Discovering Passions: Through various subjects and activities, you may discover new interests and passions. Whether it's science, sports, art, or technology, education exposes you to a world of possibilities.

Developing Social Skills: School is a place where you meet new people and learn to work with others. Group projects, discussions, and extracurricular activities help you build teamwork and communication skills, essential for life.

6. Creating Informed Citizens

Education plays a vital role in shaping responsible and informed citizens:

Understanding Society: Education teaches you about the world, history, and different cultures. This knowledge helps you understand current events and your place in society.

Being Involved: An educated individual is more likely to participate in community activities, vote, and engage in discussions about important issues. Education empowers you to make a difference in your community and beyond.

Education is a powerful force that shapes who we are and what we can achieve. It provides knowledge, builds critical thinking skills, boosts confidence, opens up opportunities, promotes personal growth, and helps create informed citizens. Remember, education is a journey that lasts a lifetime. So embrace it with curiosity, enthusiasm, and an open heart, and watch how it transforms your life!

CHAPTER 8:Fun Activities

Test Your Knowledge About Alex Karp!
Are you ready to see how much you know about Alex Karp, the co-founder and CEO of Palantir Technologies? Take this fun quiz to test your knowledge! Each question has multiple-choice answers. Good luck!
Question 1: Where was Alex Karp born?

---

a) California
b) New York
c) Pennsylvania
d) Texas
Question 2: What company did Alex Karp co-found?

---

a) Microsoft

b) Palantir Technologies

c) Google

d) Apple

Question 3: What is Palantir primarily known for?

---

a) Video games

b) Data analysis and software

c) Fashion design

d) Automobile manufacturing

Question 4: What does Alex believe is essential for turning mistakes into successes?

---

a) Ignoring them

b) Learning from them

c) Hiding them

d) Blaming others

Question 5: Which of the following is one of Alex Karp's key pieces of advice for young dreamers?

---

a) Don't take risks

b) Always follow the crowd

c) Believe in yourself

d) Stay in your comfort zone

Question 6: How does Alex Karp view failure?

a) As something to be ashamed of
b) As a learning opportunity
c) As a reason to give up
d) As a sign of weakness

Question 7: What skill does Alex emphasize as important for young people to develop?

a) Cooking
b) Critical thinking
c) Gardening
d) Sports

Question 8: What is one of Alex Karp's values when working with his team?

a) Isolation
b) Collaboration
c) Competition
d) Perfectionism

Answers Key
c) Pennsylvania
b) Palantir Technologies
b) Data analysis and software
b) Learning from them

c) Believe in yourself
b) As a learning opportunity
b) Critical thinking
b) Collaboration
Create Your Own Business Idea

Are you ready to unleash your creativity and come up with your own business idea? Starting a business can be a fun and exciting way to turn your interests and passions into something amazing. Here's a guide to help you brainstorm and create your own unique business idea!

Step 1: Identify Your Interests and Passions

Think about what you love to do. What are your hobbies? What activities make you happy? Here are some questions to get you started:

What subjects do you enjoy in school? (e.g., art, science, sports)

Do you have any special talents? (e.g., drawing, singing, coding)

What problems do you notice around you? (e.g., waste, boredom, lack of fun activities)

Step 2: Brainstorm Business Ideas

Now that you know your interests, it's time to brainstorm some business ideas! Here are a few categories to inspire you:

Service-Based Business: Think about services you could offer to help others.

Example: Dog walking, tutoring, lawn care, or babysitting.

Product-Based Business: Create or sell a product that people would enjoy.

Example: Handmade crafts, custom t-shirts, or delicious baked goods.

Tech Business: Use technology to create something cool!

Example: An app for organizing homework, a website for sharing stories, or a game.

Sustainable Business: Focus on helping the environment.

Example: A recycling service, eco-friendly products, or a garden care service.

Creative Business: Share your artistic talents with the world.

Example: Art classes, online tutorials, or personalized illustrations.

Step 3: Choose Your Target Audience

Decide who your business will serve. This could be kids, adults, pet owners, students, or anyone else who might benefit from your product or service.

Example: If you want to start a baking business, your target audience could be families looking for birthday cakes or treats for special occasions.

Step 4: Make a Business Plan

Creating a simple business plan can help you organize your ideas. Here's what to include:

Business Name: What will you call your business? Make it catchy and easy to remember!

Description: What will you offer? Describe your products or services in a few sentences.

Location: Where will you operate? Will you sell online, at a market, or from home?

Marketing: How will you let people know about your business? Think about social media, flyers, or word-of-mouth.

Goals: What do you hope to achieve? Set a few short-term and long-term goals for your business.

Step 5: Get Started!

Once you have your idea and plan, it's time to take action:

Start Small: You don't have to launch a big business right away. Start with a small project or a few customers to test your idea.

Ask for Help: Don't hesitate to ask friends, family, or teachers for support. They can offer advice or help you spread the word.

Have Fun: Remember that creating a business should be enjoyable! Stay motivated and have fun while working on your idea.

Example Business Idea: Eco-Friendly Snack Box

Business Name: Green Snack Box

Description: An eco-friendly subscription service that delivers healthy, organic snacks to kids. Each box is packed with delicious treats that are good for the planet!

Target Audience: Health-conscious families looking for convenient snack options for their children.

Location: Online subscription model with deliveries to customers' homes.

Marketing: Use social media platforms like Instagram and Facebook to showcase the snacks and promote a healthy lifestyle. Collaborate with local schools to offer free samples.

Goals:

Short-term: Launch the first box within three months and get 50 subscribers.

Long-term: Expand the product range and partner with local farmers to source ingredients.

CHAPTER 9: Alex Karp's Legacy

What Can We Learn from Alex Karp?

Alex Karp, the co-founder and CEO of Palantir Technologies, is an inspiring figure who has shown us that with determination, creativity, and a focus on teamwork, we can achieve great things. Here are some important lessons we can learn from Alex Karp's journey that can inspire us in our own lives.

1. Embrace Curiosity

Never Stop Learning: Alex believes in the power of curiosity. He encourages everyone to ask questions, explore new ideas, and seek knowledge. Being curious helps you discover new interests and can lead to amazing opportunities.

Explore Different Fields: Alex studied various subjects, including philosophy and law, before becoming a tech entrepreneur. This shows us that exploring different areas can enrich our understanding and creativity.

2. Learn from Failure

Mistakes are Valuable: Alex emphasizes that failure is not the end; it's a chance to learn. When things don't go as planned, it's important to analyze what went wrong and use that knowledge to improve.

Resilience is Key: The ability to bounce back from setbacks is crucial. Each time you face a challenge, remember that it's an opportunity to grow stronger and smarter.

3. The Power of Teamwork

Collaboration Over Competition: Alex believes that working together is essential for success. He values diverse perspectives and ideas that come from teamwork. When we collaborate with others, we can achieve more than we could alone.

Communicate and Share Ideas: Effective communication is vital in any team. Sharing thoughts and listening to others can lead to better solutions and innovations.

4. Think Big and Innovate

Challenge the Norms: Alex encourages us to think outside the box. Don't be afraid to come up with bold ideas that might seem unusual at first. Innovation often comes from trying something new and different.

Focus on Solving Problems: Whether in business or daily life, identifying problems and coming up with creative solutions can make a positive impact. Ask yourself, "What problem am I trying to solve?" and let that guide your efforts.

5. Stay True to Your Values

Integrity Matters: Alex is known for his strong values and ethical stance. Staying true to your principles, even when faced with tough decisions, builds trust and respect from others.

Make a Difference: Think about how you can use your skills and knowledge to help others and make the world a better place. Whether it's through your career or personal projects, making a positive impact is a worthwhile goal.

6. Vision for the Future

Have a Clear Vision: Alex emphasizes the importance of having a vision for what you want to achieve. A clear goal helps you stay focused and motivated, guiding your decisions along the way.

Adapt and Evolve: The world is constantly changing, and it's important to be adaptable. Stay open to new ideas and be willing to adjust your plans as necessary to keep moving forward.

Alex Karp's journey teaches us valuable lessons about curiosity, resilience, teamwork, innovation, integrity, and vision. By embracing these principles, we can inspire ourselves and others to pursue our dreams and make a positive impact in the world. Remember, every great achievement starts with a simple idea and the determination to see it through! So go ahead, dream big, and take the first step toward your own amazing journey!

How to Follow Your Dreams

Following your dreams is an exciting adventure that can lead to great achievements and personal fulfillment. Whether your dream is to become an artist, a scientist, an athlete, or anything else, here's a step-by-step guide to help you turn your dreams into reality!

1. Identify Your Dreams

Think About What You Love: Take some time to reflect on your passions and interests. What activities make you feel happy and excited? Write down your dreams, no matter how big or small.

Be Specific: Instead of just saying, "I want to be an artist," try to specify what type of artist you want to be. Do you want to paint, draw comics, or create digital art? The more specific you are, the clearer your path will become.

2. Set Goals

Create Short-Term and Long-Term Goals: Break down your big dream into smaller, achievable goals. Short-term goals can be things you want to accomplish in the next few weeks or months, while long-term goals might take years to achieve.

Write Your Goals Down: Writing your goals helps you remember them and makes them feel more real. You can create a vision board or a goal journal to keep track of your progress.

3. Make a Plan

Create a Step-by-Step Plan: Outline the steps you need to take to reach your goals. What skills do you need to develop? What resources or materials will you require?

Be Flexible: Sometimes, your plan might need adjustments along the way. Be open to changing your approach if you encounter obstacles or discover new interests.

4. Take Action

Start Small: Begin with the first step in your plan, even if it seems minor. Every little action you take gets you closer to your dream.

Stay Consistent: Keep working toward your goals regularly. Even small, daily efforts can lead to significant progress over time.

5. Stay Motivated

Surround Yourself with Support: Share your dreams with family and friends who will encourage you. Join groups or communities of like-minded people who share your interests and passions.

Celebrate Small Wins: Acknowledge and celebrate your achievements, no matter how small they may seem. This will boost your confidence and keep you motivated.

6. Learn and Improve

Seek Knowledge: Continuously learn about your dream. Read books, take classes, watch tutorials, or find a mentor who can guide you.

Embrace Challenges: Don't be afraid of setbacks. Challenges are a natural part of the journey, and they often help you grow. Learn from mistakes and use them to improve.

7. Stay Positive

Maintain a Positive Attitude: Believe in yourself and your abilities. Positive thinking can help you overcome obstacles and keep you focused on your dreams.

Visualize Your Success: Imagine yourself achieving your dream. Visualization can be a powerful tool to motivate you and keep you inspired.

8. Keep Dreaming Big

Don't Limit Yourself: Your dreams may change over time, and that's okay! As you grow and learn, allow yourself to dream even bigger.

Stay Curious: Explore new interests and opportunities. You never know what might spark a new passion or lead you in a different direction.

Following your dreams is a journey filled with excitement, challenges, and growth. By identifying your dreams, setting goals, creating a plan, and taking action, you can turn your aspirations into reality. Remember, it's okay to encounter bumps along the road—every step you take brings you closer to your dreams. So go out there, believe in yourself, and start pursuing the life you've always dreamed of!

Glossary of Terms

Key Words to Know

When pursuing your dreams and exploring new ideas, it's helpful to understand some key terms that can guide you along the way. Here are some important words related to following your dreams, along with their meanings:

1. Dream

Definition: A dream is a desire or aspiration for the future. It's what you hope to achieve or become.

Example: "My dream is to become a doctor and help people."

2. Goal

Definition: A goal is a specific target or outcome you want to achieve. Goals can be short-term (quick wins) or long-term (bigger dreams).

Example: "I have a goal to read one book every month."

3. Plan

Definition: A plan is a detailed strategy for how to achieve your goals. It outlines the steps you need to take.

Example: "I made a plan to practice my soccer skills every Saturday."

4. Action

Definition: Action refers to the steps you take to make your goals happen. It's about doing things rather than just thinking about them.

Example: "Taking action means working on my art every day."

5. Motivation

Definition: Motivation is the drive or reason behind why you want to achieve something. It's what keeps you going, even when things get tough.

Example: "My motivation for studying hard is to get into a good college."

6. Resilience

Definition: Resilience is the ability to bounce back from challenges or setbacks. It's about staying strong and not giving up.

Example: "Her resilience helped her overcome obstacles in her path."

7. Vision

Definition: A vision is a clear picture of what you want to achieve in the future. It helps guide your goals and actions.

Example: "My vision is to create a world where everyone has access to clean water."

8. Passion

Definition: Passion is a strong feeling of enthusiasm or love for something. It drives you to pursue your interests.

Example: "I have a passion for dancing that inspires me to practice every day."

9. Persistence

Definition: Persistence is the quality of continuing to try despite difficulties. It's about keeping on until you reach your goal.

Example: "His persistence in practicing the guitar paid off when he performed at the school concert."

10. Achievement

Definition: An achievement is something you accomplish, especially after a lot of effort. It's a goal that you have successfully reached.

Example: "Winning the science fair was a big achievement for her."

Conclusion

Understanding these keywords can help you navigate your journey toward following your dreams. Each term represents an important aspect of setting goals and achieving success. As you continue on your path, remember to embrace these concepts, and they will guide you along the way!

Understanding Technology and Business

In today's world, technology and business go hand in hand. Understanding how they work together can help you see the amazing ways technology can improve businesses and everyday life. Let's break it down into simple parts so you can see why this is important!

1. What is Technology?

Definition: Technology includes all the tools, machines, and systems that help us do things faster and more efficiently. It can be anything from computers and smartphones to the internet and robotics.

Examples:

Computers help us create documents and presentations.
Smartphones let us communicate with friends and access information quickly.
The internet connects people around the globe, making information easily accessible.

2. What is Business?

Definition: Business refers to any activity that involves producing goods or providing services to earn money. It can be a small shop, a large corporation, or even a freelancer working from home.

Examples:

A bakery sells bread and pastries to customers.

A software company develops apps to help people with their daily tasks.

A farmer grows fruits and vegetables to sell at the market.

3. How Technology Impacts Business

Efficiency: Technology helps businesses operate more efficiently. For example, using computers and software can speed up tasks like accounting and inventory management.

Communication: With technology, businesses can communicate quickly and easily with customers and employees. Emails, video calls, and messaging apps make it simple to stay in touch.

Marketing: Businesses can reach a wider audience through online marketing. Social media, websites, and digital advertising allow companies to promote their products or services effectively.

Data Analysis: Technology enables businesses to collect and analyze data to make informed decisions. By understanding customer preferences, companies can improve their products and services.

Innovation: Technology drives innovation, helping businesses create new products and services. For example, electric cars and smart home devices are products born from technological advancements.

4. The Role of Technology in Different Industries

Healthcare: Technology in healthcare includes telemedicine, electronic health records, and medical devices that help doctors diagnose and treat patients more effectively.

Education: Technology enhances learning through online courses, educational apps, and interactive tools that make studying more engaging.

Entertainment: Streaming services, video games, and social media platforms have transformed how we enjoy entertainment, allowing for easy access to content.

Transportation: Technology has improved transportation with GPS, ride-sharing apps, and electric vehicles, making it easier to travel and transport goods.

5. The Importance of Learning About Technology in Business

Career Opportunities: Many jobs today require some knowledge of technology. Learning about technology can help you find exciting career opportunities in various fields.

Entrepreneurship: If you dream of starting your own business, understanding technology can give you an advantage. You can use tech tools to create and grow your business effectively.

Adaptability: The world is constantly changing, and technology evolves rapidly. Learning about technology helps you adapt to new trends and stay competitive.

Made in United States
Troutdale, OR
05/25/2025